Zeus And Prometheus

Augusta Larned

Kessinger Publishing's Rare Reprints

Thousands of Scarce and Hard-to-Find Books on These and other Subjects!

- Americana
- Ancient Mysteries
- Animals
- Anthropology
- Architecture
- Arts
- Astrology
- Bibliographies
- Biographies & Memoirs
- Body, Mind & Spirit
- Business & Investing
- Children & Young Adult
- Collectibles
- Comparative Religions
- Crafts & Hobbies
- Earth Sciences
- Education
- Ephemera
- Fiction
- Folklore
- Geography
- Health & Diet
- History
- Hobbies & Leisure
- Humor
- Illustrated Books
- Language & Culture
- Law
- Life Sciences
- Literature
- Medicine & Pharmacy
- Metaphysical
- Music
- Mystery & Crime
- Mythology
- Natural History
- Outdoor & Nature
- Philosophy
- Poetry
- Political Science
- Science
- Psychiatry & Psychology
- Reference
- Religion & Spiritualism
- Rhetoric
- Sacred Books
- Science Fiction
- Science & Technology
- Self-Help
- Social Sciences
- Symbolism
- Theatre & Drama
- Theology
- Travel & Explorations
- War & Military
- Women
- Yoga
- *Plus Much More!*

We kindly invite you to view our catalog list at:
http://www.kessinger.net

THIS ARTICLE WAS EXTRACTED FROM THE BOOK:

Old Tales Retold from Grecian Mythology in Talks Around the Fire

BY THIS AUTHOR:

Augusta Larned

ISBN 0766102505

READ MORE ABOUT THE BOOK AT OUR WEB SITE:

http://www.kessinger.net

OR ORDER THE COMPLETE
BOOK FROM YOUR FAVORITE STORE

ISBN 0766102505

Because this article has been extracted from a parent book, it may have non-pertinent text at the beginning or end of it.

Any blank pages following the article are necessary for our book production requirements. The article herein is complete.

THIRD EVENING.

ZEUS AND PROMETHEUS.

Jack. I have just finished this capital story of "One-eyed Tim, the Ranger," and now I am ready for a dose of mythology.

Aunt A. I am sorry if you consider it a dose.

Mother. You ought to turn him out of the room for that speech. It is not worth while to cast pearls of knowledge before such an unappreciative boy.

Jack. I am as good a listener as any of them, Aunt Abby. Just let them try to turn me out, and they will find that I have spirit if not appreciation.

Helen. Be quiet, Jack. What are you going to talk about this evening, Aunt Abby?

Aunt A. The birth of Zeus, (Jupiter,) and his brothers and sisters, and the manner in which he set up his throne on Olympus. The Titans, of whom I gave you an account, were the early race of deities, sometimes called the elder gods. When Zeus began to reign their power ceased,

Fred. But where does the creation of man come in? You have not as yet told us any thing about him.

Aunt A. In the old Greek system man was an after-thought. The earth was made originally for the gods. There is no well-defined story in regard to the way man came into being. The ancients did not believe that the human race sprang from a single pair in accordance with the Bible narrative. They held that human beings were created separately, in various places, and, like the gods, were born of Mother Earth. In hilly regions they were supposed to have sprung from rocks and trees; in valleys, from moisture. There is a story about the great Titan god, Prometheus, who, we are told, made men out of earth and water after a great deluge, called the flood of Deucalion, had swept the human race away. This will remind you of Noah's flood. When the earth was again quite bare of inhabitants, Zeus (Jupiter) ordered Prometheus and the goddess Athene (Minerva) to mold a new race out of mud, and he told the winds to breathe life into their nostrils. Prometheus is said to have given to his men something of all the qualities possessed by fishes, birds, beasts, and reptiles, so that they formed a link in the long chain of creation; and the kind of earth out of which he molded them was shown in later times at a place near Phocis.

Helen. Did he make women, too?

Aunt A. No; the first woman of mythology had a very different origin. She was, in fact, expressly created to draw down misfortunes on the head of Prometheus, the maker and friend of man.

Sue. What was her name?

Aunt A. Pandora.

Helen. Do you mean the one that unluckily opened the box, and let fly all the troubles that now fill the world?

Aunt A. Yes, the same. She was expressly created to work ill for men.

Fred. Is her story not, then, in some respects, like the account of Eve in the Bible?

Aunt A. No; only so far as she was believed to have drawn down misfortunes on the head of mankind. In this respect we may call her the Grecian Eve, but the account of her creation differs materially from the beautiful Bible narrative. The Bible represents Eve as created expressly to be the companion and helpmeet of Adam; but Pandora was designed for a curse and mischief-maker from the beginning. I shall probably mention Pandora again before the evening is through. You will remember that the Titan gods were liberated from Tartarus, where their father, Uranus, the sky, had put them for safe keeping, and how Cronus managed to dethrone old Uranus by the aid of his sickle.

Sue. O, yes; we remember all that very well.

Aunt A. Cronus then became chief ruler. He married his own sister, Rhea, an earth goddess, daughter of Mother Earth, and their children were numbered among the highest gods of the Greeks. I will give you both the Greek and Latin names of the gods until you become familiarized with them. It has been the almost universal practice to use the Latin names for Greek gods. The Romans borrowed nearly all their deities from the Greeks, and in a number of instances they changed the character and attributes of the gods they had borrowed. It is, therefore, far more correct to give to the gods their own proper names by which they were known to the Greeks, but as you are not familiar with these I will also add their equivalents, the common Latin terms.

Helen. Why were not the true Greek names used in the first place?

Aunt A. Because for a long time almost all that was known of Grecian religion was learned from Latin authors. The knowledge came filtered down through their language, and the Greek gods were first introduced to us in their Roman dress and with their Roman names. When scholars began to study Greek for themselves, they restored to the gods all that had been taken away from them. Cronus is often confounded with Saturn, a god of the Romans, but he was a very different deity. The children of Cronus and Rhea, his wife, were Aides, (Pluto,) Poseidon, (Neptune,) Hestia, (Vesta,) Demeter, (Ceres,) Hera, (Juno,) and Zeus, (Jupiter.) This constituted the powerful family of gods that finally gained control over the universe. Those who shared their power and reigned with them in Olympus were, for the most part, the children of Zeus.

Jack. How was old Cronus put out of the way?

Aunt A. It had been predicted in time past that Cronus would lose his throne by his youngest son, just as he himself had deposed his father. To prevent this disaster, he invented the ingenious mode of swallowing his children as fast as they came into the world. In this way he conveniently rid himself of five.

Fred. I thought that story was told of Saturn.

Aunt A. So it is; but the story belongs to Cronus. He and the Roman Saturn may have been originally the same, although the points of resemblance are now but few.

Helen. Was the little Jupiter swallowed, too?

Aunt A. No; he was the sixth and youngest child, and Rhea, his mother, who had with horror seen her offspring devoured, determined to save this one at all hazards. She cheated her husband very cunningly by presenting him a stone wrapped, like a new-born babe, in swaddling clothes, which he at once proceeded to swallow, but we are not told how the repast agreed with him.

Sue. Then what did Rhea do with the baby, Jupiter?

Aunt A. She had him carried secretly to a cave on Mount Ida, in the Island of Crete, and kept him there concealed. Two kind mountain nymphs, named Adrastea and Ida, took care of him, and acted as his nurses. The little bees busily gathered him honey all day long, and a friendly goat, named Amalthea, supplied him with milk. In gratitude to Amalthea

Zeus (Jupiter.)

he afterward turned her into a bright twinkling star. Cronus appears to have been a stupid, sluggish old god, very easily cheated, and to prevent him from hearing the cries of the new-born child, Rhea ordered her servants, called the Curetes, to keep up a perpetual din by clashing their swords and bucklers.

Helen. What became of the children that were swallowed? Did they remain forever inside their cruel old father?

Aunt A. By no means, and that is the strangest part of the story. Their grandmother, Gæa, (the Earth,) you will remember, was a wily old goddess. She contrived to give her son, Cronus, an emetic, which brought the children up again alive and well. The stone swallowed in place of Zeus (Jupiter) was brought to light also, and this stone Zeus afterward set up as a memorial at Delphi, near the great oracle of Apollo.

Fred. I remember you told us Cronus was called the ripener, or harvest god. Perhaps this story about the way his children were brought up means nothing more than the sprouting of seeds.

Aunt A. In that case the emetic of old Mother Gæa would be a shower of rain, or warm burst of sunshine. Cronus was certainly the harvest god, for his sickle proves that beyond a doubt. He is also used as a personification of Time, as the words "chronology" and "chronometer" imply. The unnatural father, who swallowed his own children, simply means the ingathering of the harvest. As time passes the grain that grew in summer is consumed, but when spring comes Mother Earth again causes the little seed to sprout that has long lain hidden in the dark bosom of the ground. I do not offer this as a full explanation of the myth. It is simply a hint as to its possible meaning.

Jack. I am anxious to know how Jupiter managed to get his throne.

Aunt A. The young god had excellent nursing, and grew rapidly. He soon showed vast powers of mind, and with the assistance of his strong brothers and sisters contrived to banish old Cronus to the Islands of the Blessed, where he reigned over the happy souls that were permitted to take up their abode there. This overthrow of Cronus was in accordance with the predictions of fate. Zeus seated himself on his father's throne, but it was not without a terrible struggle that he secured a peaceful reign.

Fred. Did the old gods make war on this new upstart?

Aunt A. Yes; they were indignant at his assumption of power. The Titans, those dread children of Earth and Uranus, entirely disapproved of his course. They made war upon him, and he was unable to cope with them single-handed. To assist him in the conflict he called upon all the gods, and Styx, as I have told you, was the first to come and offer her services. He also released from Tartarus, where they had been chained, those curious monsters, the Cyclops, with one round eye in the middle of the forehead, and the hundred-armed Giants, named Briareus, Cottus, and Gyges. These creatures were grateful to Zeus (Jupiter) for setting them free, and made him a present of thunder and lightning, which he ever after held in his hand and hurled from his high throne on Olympus down upon the earth beneath. The conflict was fierce and terrible. We are told it lasted nine years. But, by the aid of these allies, and the assistance of his own brothers and sisters, he succeeded in casting his defeated enemies again down into Tartarus.

Fred. If Zeus, or Jupiter, was obliged to seek so much help in overcoming his enemies, the Greeks could not have thought him all-powerful.

Aunt A. No; they evidently did not. He was thwarted in his plans and wishes many times by the wiles and deceit of other gods, but he came nearer to the one truly just, all-wise, and good Providence than any idea those ancient people who were groping for the light of divine things had ever formed.

Helen. Now he had overcome the Titans, was he secure on his throne?

Aunt A. No. His grandmother Gæa, that vindictive and restless old goddess, was highly indignant at the fate which had overtaken her sons, the Titans, for whom she had a doting fondness. Therefore she stirred up another set of her offspring, called the Giants, to rebel against Zeus. They piled up mountains and rocks for the purpose of climbing into heaven. This was a very poetical way of accounting for the savage wildness of mountainous regions. Those ancient men were quite content to think it the work of angry monsters, who were trying to pull down Zeus from his high seat in heaven. You will be reminded by this story of the Tower of Babel, built on the plain of Shinar, not by ferocious gods, but by ambitious men. Zeus (Jupiter) hurled his new thunder forth without terrifying or injuring his terrible assailants. His brothers and sisters did their very best to help him, but all in vain until the great hero Heracles took sides with the defenders. By his might he slew some of the giants, and dashed others down into deep chasms, where he buried them under rocks and mountains.

Helen. Was this the end of the war?

Aunt A. No. Defeat only seemed to stir up old Gæa to greater activity. She thirsted for vengeance, and called out of Tartarus a monster of monsters named Typhœus, whom I have already described to you. So terrible was the battle between Zeus and Typhœus, Olympus rocked wildly on its base — heaven, and earth, and sea were boiling like a huge caldron. A horrible din filled the universe. Even Aides, (Pluto,) monarch of the under world, sat and quaked at the sound, and the Titans in black Tartarus were terribly frightened. It seemed as though the end of creation was at hand. Some of the gods fled to Egypt in their fright, and were transformed into fishes in the river Nile. Typhœus was finally conquered by one of Zeus's thunderbolts, that scorched his numerous heads with lightning, and was afterward buried in Mount Ætna.

Sue. Did he make the volcano?

Aunt A. Yes, so it was thought. The monster was supposed to lie flat upon his back with the Island of Sicily, anciently known as Trinacia, heaped over him; his right hand was placed beneath the Ansonian Pelorus, now called Cape de Faro; his left under Pachynus, now Cape Passaro; his legs were held down by Lilybæum, now known as Cape Masala. Ætna was planted directly upon his head, and the monster continually vomited forth flames and burning lava through the mouth of the volcano. When he struggled to throw off the load of earth the ground was shaken by earthquakes, cities were toppled down, and huge mountains moved from their foundations.

Fred. That was an ingenious way of accounting for earthquakes.

Aunt A. Yes, and a highly poetical explanation. Sicily is a volcanic island often shaken by earthquakes. It is far more pleasing to the fancy to think of a buried giant struggling to throw off the burden of rocks and mountains, than of the action of fire and water somewhere under ground.

Fred. I suppose the Greeks thought that all the

precipices, and chasms, and crags in their mountains were made by the war with the Titans.

Aunt A. The sides of Mount Olympus in Thessaly are wild and broken. They bristle with sharp crags, and are shaggy with thick forests. It was here that the war with the Titans took place. And, perhaps, a believing Greek could point out the very rocks the assailants hurled upon each other, and the crags and hills under which Heracles at last succeeded in burying the Giants. Those frightful Giants and Titans, we know well, were nothing more than personifications of storms, floods, tempests, hurricanes, and earthquakes, that in that southern climate often convulsed the sky, and tore the bosom of the earth.

Helen. I remember you told us Uranus means sky. Was Zeus also a sky god?

Aunt A. Zeus means the pure, clear light of day. Therefore he warred with the powers of darkness. He also stands for spiritual light and elevation in contrast to those rude, sluggish clods of earth, mere forces of nature, immoral and blind, that made up the elder gods. There was a better order of things, a higher thought about the ruler of the world when Zeus (Jupiter) came to the throne of Olympus.

Fred. I have somewhere read that the name of God in many languages means sky or light.

Aunt A. The blue heaven, so vast and serene, is an almost universal symbol of a divine Father and ruler, who clasps the world in his all-embracing arms, and smiles down with peace and love into the hearts of his children.

Helen. Was that dreadful Typhœus the last enemy Zeus had to conquer?

Aunt A. Yes. His throne was then secure. There is at least one attempt at rebellion against him afterward spoken of, but it was easily put down, and did not lead to war in heaven.

Fred. What became of his grandfather and father, Uranus and Cronus. Being immortal gods, I suppose they could not die.

Aunt A. Did I not tell you they were banished to Tartarus, where they held a kind of court in the under world, surrounded by the Titan gods, except those reserved for special punishment? Some poets make Cronus King of the Elysian Fields, or Islands of the Blessed.

Jack. I remember you told us that Prometheus was a Titan.

Aunt A. He is classed among them, although he was only the son of a Titan. His name means forethought, and that of his brother Epimetheus, afterthought. Poor Epimetheus proved that he was correctly named. His blunders brought down a great misfortune on mankind. Prometheus was the son of Iapetus and Clymene, a lovely ocean nymph. He is sometimes called a demi-god, and he was certainly the noblest and most renowned of all the Titans. His brother, Atlas, was the leader of the elder gods in their war on Zeus, and for this he was doomed to hold the sky on his shoulders. He is sometimes confounded with a huge mountain of the same name, that seems to support heaven with its head. Prometheus showed vast intellect and courage, and deathless hatred to the new king of heaven, and equal devotion to the interests of men, whom he is said to have created. He was the first god that loved mortals and wished to bless them.

Helen. I remember he stole fire from heaven, and made a present of it to men.

Aunt A. It was because of the enmity of Zeus (Jupiter) that he was obliged to steal it. Once we are told gods and men were assembled together at a place called Mecone, and were contending. It would seem that the gods demanded more than mankind were willing to grant in the way of sacrifices, and that each were trying to get the better of the other. Prometheus, the friend of the human race, took their part. He was very crafty, and having divided a huge ox in a very skillful manner, he set it before Zeus, (Jupiter.) He had made two piles. In one he placed the flesh and entrails, the fat and hide, and neatly covered it over with the stomach, a poor and worthless part. In the other he put the bones, and concealed them with a thick layer of fat, which gave the heap a rich and tempting appearance. Zeus suspected the cheat, and rebuked Prometheus; but the Titan god laughed, and said gayly, " Most glorious and renowned Zeus, greatest of living gods, choose which of these two portions you will accept." Zeus was enraged, and though not really taken in by the trick, he chose the worthless half, and when he had lifted up the fat, behold, there was nothing but bones underneath. Then he vowed in his heart to bring evils on the tribes of men, for he knew that Prometheus loved them, and that he could in this manner effectually wreak vengeance on his enemy.

Jack. How was Zeus injured by the trick Prometheus played on him?

Aunt A. It fixed the nature of sacrifices, and forever after the Greeks were accustomed to burn the bones of victims upon the altars of their gods; the flesh they reserved for their own feasts. To punish Prometheus for his deceit and the disrespect he had shown to the chief god, Zeus took away fire from men. A moment's reflection will show you that fire is indispensable to every work of progress and improvement. Only the very lowest savages, those but one step removed from the brute, are found to dispense with it for cooking their food and carrying on the affairs of life. Prometheus knew that if man ever improved, ever rose above the condition of wild beasts, that hide in caves and dens of the earth, he must have the great civilizer, fire, to help him. So, according to Hesiod, he again cheated Zeus, and stole the beautiful flame in a hollow fennel stalk from the sun. Another story tells us that, with splendid audacity, he filched fire from the hearth of Zeus in his golden house in Olympus; and still another, that he snatched it from the forge of Hephæstor, (Vulcan,) the divine smith.

Sue. Why did Prometheus love men?

Aunt A. He was a demigod—half god, as the word means—and stood in an intermediate position between gods and men. His sympathies inclined him wholly to the race of mortals he is said to have created. He belonged to the old order of things. His grandfather, Uranus, was the first ruler of the universe; therefore he naturally hated the new, and what seemed to him upstart, government of Zeus, which had imprisoned most of his own relatives in Tartarus. He rebelled against the tyranny of the new king of heaven and ranged himself with mankind, toward whom Zeus had shown no marks of favor. The old Greek poets represent him as the first great civilizer imbued with an ardent love of humanity. They tell us that he taught men a knowledge of carpentry and the art of building houses. Before that they had lived in holes, and hollow trees, and the dens of wild beasts. He instructed them how to measure and distinguish the seasons one from another, by noting the rising and setting of the stars. He imparted to them the art of numbering and of writing, and how to yoke animals to chariots and fit sails to ships.

Fred. I should like to know the meaning of the quarrel between Prometheus and Zeus.

Aunt A. It is difficult to explain. The old Greeks

always held that the gods were friendly to certain individuals and races, and very unfriendly to others. The favorite of one god might be disliked and hated by another; therefore a struggle was always going on to secure good fortune for him, or to take it away. This was the only means they had of explaining the varying fortunes of men, that sometimes bring happiness and sometimes misery. The old myth shows Zeus as an enemy to mankind, though his character was afterward changed to that of the just and benevolent ruler of the world. Prometheus, in those early ages, was man's protector and benefactor, and the whole story seems to resolve itself into the conflict between good and evil.

Helen. Tell us how poor Prometheus was punished.

Aunt A. Zeus showed himself terribly vindictive and revengeful. To punish Prometheus for the theft of fire, he ordered Hephæstos (Vulcan) to chain him to a pillar, or, according to some writers, to a rock on Mount Caucasus. The eagle of Zeus came and devoured his liver in the daytime, and it grew again during the night; but, in spite of the anguish of his martyrdom, he endured it with a steadfast mind. Prometheus is the most heroic figure of mythology. The way he bore his torture was truly sublime. Poets will never cease to depict the old Titan god, with his mighty heart undaunted, his vast will unbent, chained to the lonely rock on a wild and desolate mountain side, while that terrible bird gnawed his body. Storms swept over him, the sun scorched him, the cold froze him, but he would not yield to the tyrant. In his keeping was a prophecy of the greatest importance to Zeus. It was made by those grim Fates that sat behind the throne of the king. Prometheus knew that if Zeus married a certain goddess a son would be born of the union who was destined to dethrone his father. Zeus knew of the prophecy, but he did not know the name of the goddess; that secret was in the keeping of Prometheus, his hated foe. Zeus was in great dread of the danger which threatened him. Hermes, (Mercury,) the errand boy of the gods, was dispatched to extort the secret from the tortured Titan, but he steadily refused to render it up, preferring rather to endure the unspeakable torture than bend his mind to his foe.

Sue. Did he stay there chained to the rock forever?

Aunt A. According to some writers Prometheus was at first fastened to a rock in Scythia, and upon his refusal to tell the name of the goddess was shot, rock and all, into Tartarus by one of Zeus's thunderbolts. After the lapse of a long period, ages, perhaps, he was brought back to the upper air, and chained to the craggy side of the Caucasus. The eagle was then sent to torture him. He was doomed to continue in this state of suffering until some other god should voluntarily take his place, and descend for him into Tartarus. This happened when a good Centaur, (a being half man, half horse,) named Chiron, had been incurably wounded by the hero Heracles, and wished to retire into the lower world. According to another account Zeus himself released Prometheus when, at last, he had made known to him that the child of the sea goddess, Thetis, if he should marry her, would deprive him of his power.

Helen. You remember, Aunt Abby, you were to tell us about the creation of Pandora, the first woman.

Aunt A. I have just come to Pandora, for she forms an important part of the story of Prometheus, and the singular hatred of Zeus for the human race. Zeus, you will remember, wished to destroy mankind, and put an entirely different order of beings in their place. Prometheus frustrated this design by stealing fire from heaven. Then Zeus set to work to devise mischief for men. He ordered Hephæstos, (Vulcan,) the divine artist, who worked in gold, bronze, clay, or whatever came to his hand, to mold out of earth the image of a modest, beautiful maiden. This was the first woman, Pandora. We are not told that a soul was given her, but are left to infer that she was destitute of that appendage. On the other hand many of the gods and goddesses brought gifts to this wonderful new creature. She was furnished with a long list of graces, charms, and fascinations. Great Athene, (Minerva,) goddess of wisdom, dressed her in a shining white robe, and covered her head with a vail of exquisite embroidery. Hephæstos (Vulcan) made for her a golden crown, with various figures of sea monsters. Athene (Minerva) taught her how to work and weave beautiful webs. Aphrodite (Venus) shed grace upon her head. Cunning Hermes (Mercury) endowed her with deceit, and with enticing manners. The lovely Graces and the goddess Persuasion hung golden chains about her neck and limbs, and delightful rosy Hours crowned her with fresh spring blossoms. Her beautiful ornaments were only exceeded by her charms of person.

Fred. I suppose she was made on purpose to bewitch and cheat men.

Aunt A. The first created woman in the Bible was pure, and good, and lovely. She fell into sin because she was tempted; but the first woman of Greek mythology was made deceitful, and crafty, and full of guile. The old poet calls her a beauteous evil. When she was led out into the world wonder and delight seized upon the minds of men. Prometheus, whose name meant forethought, and who was very long-headed, had charged his brother Epimetheus, blundering after-thought, not to accept any present from Zeus, (Jupiter,) for gifts from an enemy are always to be distrusted. Wily Hermes (Mercury) led Pandora to Epimetheus, who, true to his name, forgot all about his brother's warning, and the danger of receiving her, until it was too late. He was trans ported by her beauty and grace, and took her into his house and made her his wife.

Jack. What about her wonderful box?

Aunt A. Instead of a Saratoga trunk filled with finery, Pandora carried to the house of her husband a vase, or box, containing all the evils that afflict the world; such as trouble, pain, weariness, care, disease, sin, death. The lid was to remain forever closed, but, tempted by curiosity, Epimetheus uncovered his wife's box, and out flew a host of horrible ills, leaving nothing behind but deceitful hope.

Jack. Grecian mythology agrees with the Bible in laying all the trouble there is in the world to the first woman.

Helen. I don't see it in that way. It was male curiosity that did the mischief. I don't believe Pandora would ever have opened the box, but Epimetheus couldn't let it alone, and then, probably, he charged the fault on her. Men always say that women are at the bottom of every trouble.

Aunt A. If a woman does the mischief, as in the case of Pandora, she always finds a man to help her, some weak-minded Epimetheus who cannot resist temptation.

This is the end of this publication.

Any remaining blank pages are for our book binding requirements and are blank on purpose.

To search thousands of interesting publications like this one, please remember to visit our website at:

http://www.kessinger.net

CPSIA information can be obtained
at www.ICGtesting.com
Printed in the USA
LVHW090004210720
661165LV00008B/128